GOLF IN THE COMIC STRIPS

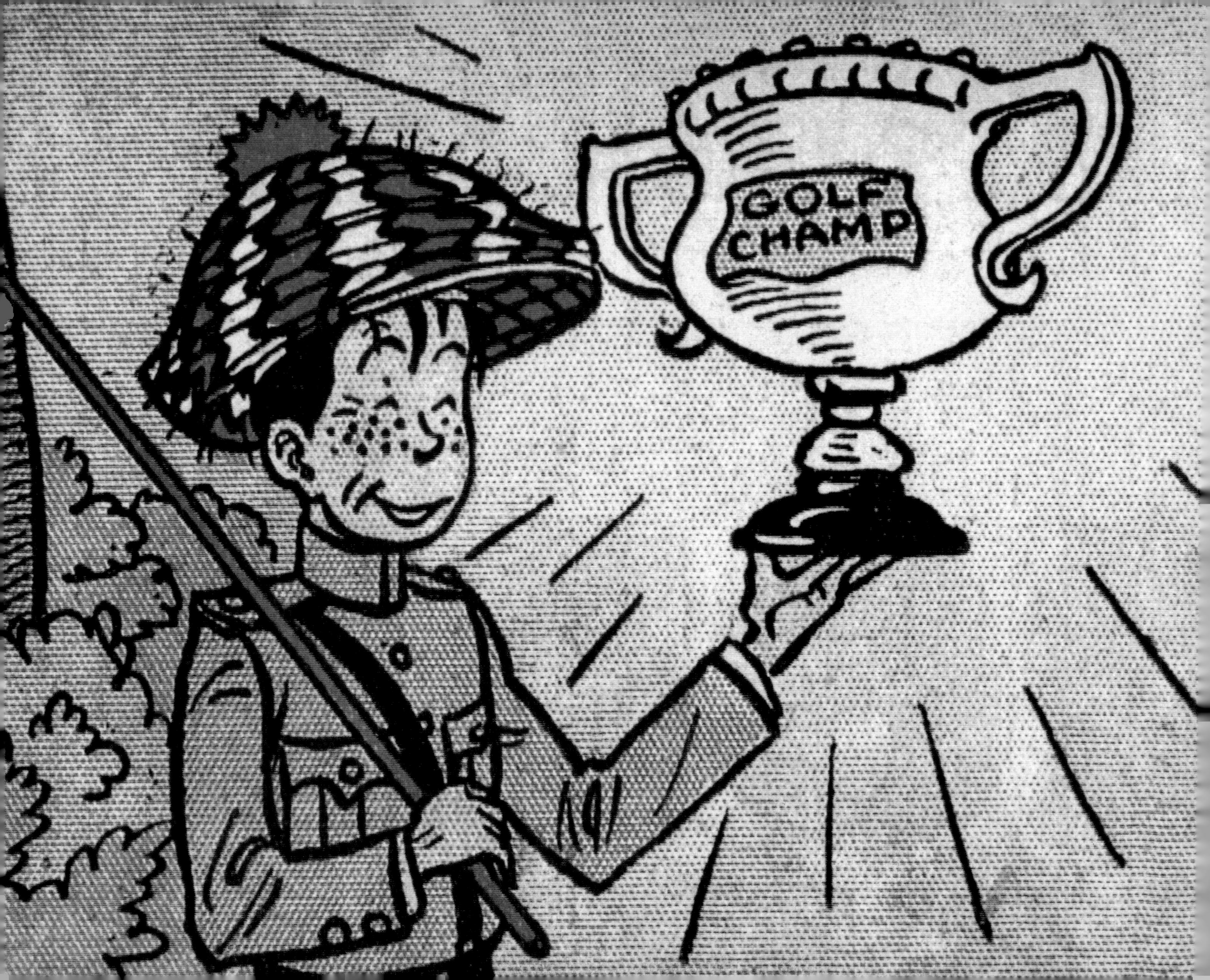
GOLF
CHAMP

GOLF IN THE COMIC STRIPS

A HISTORIC COLLECTION
OF CLASSIC CARTOONS

By Howard Ziehm

"Fore" word by Bob Hope

General Publishing Group, Inc.

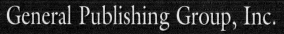

Publisher: W. Quay Hays
Art Director: Kurt Wahlner
Managing Editor: Colby Allerton
Production Director: Trudihope Schlomowitz
Color and Pre-Press Manager: Bill Castillo
Production Artist: Gaston Moraga
Production Assistants: David Chadderdon, Tom Archibeque, Gus Dawson
Copy Editor: Steve Baeck

RT JM

For Information:
General Publishing Group, Inc.
2701 Ocean Park Boulevard
Santa Monica, CA 90405

Library of Congress Cataloging-in-Publication Data

Golf in the comic strips / [edited] by Howard Ziehm.
     p.   cm.
   ISBN 1-57544-053-9
   1. Golf—Comic books, strips, etc. I. Ziehm, Howard.
PN6726.G57   1997
741.5'973—dc21   97-3924
                                                      CIP

Frontispiece: General Halftrack, in *Beetle Bailey*, by
Mort Walker, 1990 (reprinted with special
permission of King Features Syndicate)

Flyleaf, left: Blackie, in *Ella Cinders*,
by Conselman & Plumb, 1929

Flyleaf, right: *The Captain and the Kids*,
by Rudolph Dirks, 1922

Printed in the USA by
RR Donnelley & Sons Company
10 9 8 7 6 5 4 3 2 1

Back cover, upper right: Reprinted with permission
of Johnny Hart and Creators Syndicate Inc.

Back flap: Reprinted with permission of Tribune
Media Service.

ACKNOWLEDGMENTS

Although the material for this book was garnered from the tedious hours I spent poring through microfilm of American newspapers, many people have contributed to the final presentation.

First I would like to thank Bill Blackbeard and the San Francisco Museum of Comic Art for supplying copies of all the historical color sheets. Without that source putting this book together would have been a difficult task. I also want to thank two libraries in California: Santa Monica Public Library and the UCLA Research Library. Being able to work for countless hours on high-quality microfilm readers with copying capability was essential to my project. It is a credit to those libraries that this equipment is available. I would also like to thank Professor Lucy Caswell and the Ohio State University Library of Graphic Arts for allowing me to peruse through their material while I was attending the Comic Strip Festival held at OSU in 1995. Beyond finding strips in the library's collection, I was exposed to three days of contact with some of the best cartoonists in America today.

I would like to thank Frank D'Angelo of King Features and Mort Walker for giving me encouragement to continue with the project. Positive input is essential to completing a task such as this. I am grateful to all the syndicates for working with me to make their material available at a financially reasonable price. I would especially like to thank Elizabeth Nolan of King Features for guiding me to the right source for material whose ownership was difficult to ascertain.

I am most indebted to Quay Hays, publisher of General Publishing Group, for undertaking this project and providing the staff to put it together. Although many publishers found the book titillating, it took a bit of a maverick to make it happen. I also want to thank my agent and, in particular, Annette Trotta of Monaco, Leonne and Trotta for working out a deal that could make the book a reality. With all the rights that had to be obtained, this was not an easy task. Thanks are in order to Kurt Wahlner, the art director at GPG who supervised the overall layout and the design of the title pages, Colby Allerton who made sure the text made sense, and Vera Matranga and Maritta Tapanainen for adding color to selected strips.

I want to thank my friend Ray Pachette, who worked many all-night sessions on his computer restoring the microfilm copies to print quality. I would also like to express gratitude to Ron Muszalski of Cambridge Golf Antiquities at Pebble Beach for his heartfelt encouragement and effort in finding original material and background material on some of the artists.

I am most appreciative of the attention I was given by Beverly Gosnell, writer for the *Malibu Surfside* and golf partner at the Kiwanis tournament, and Geana Channel of *Who's Who*, a cable show in Malibu. Because of Beverly I attended the OSU event, and Geana has allowed me to present *Golf in the Comic Strips* several times on her TV show. I also want to thank my golfing pal, Mike Karg, for his enthusiastic support of this project and the promotion of golftoons in general; Frank Springer, president of the National Cartoonist's Society for helping me locate syndicators; and Richard Olsen of the Outcault Society for information on the works of the inventor of the comic strip.

Finally I want to thank my wife of 24 years, Judy, for taping to the refrigerator door—and leaving it there—*The Wizard of Id* of 1982 that was the inspiration that led me to begin this project nine years later.

Full credit to the owners of copyright accompanies each strip not in public domain. With some of the older drawings, copyright confusion still exists; and a few individuals and organizations seem to have dropped out of sight altogether. If in our credits we have fallen short of legal perfection, we extend apologies. Our efforts to trace copyright owners were strenuous and if errors or omissions exist we shall be happy to correct them in later editions.

"FORE" WORD

I'm truly honored to be asked to write a foreword to a book about golf. I've had a lifelong love affair with the game...well, 70 years anyway. You see, golf has been my real racket. Entertainment has just been a sideline. I tell jokes to pay my green fees.

Golf is the greatest game in the world and on a good day, in the company of a willing pigeon, a most lucrative game. Golf at times can be a frustrating and humbling experience, and Howard Ziehm's book is testimony that golf is also the funniest game in the world.

Rule number one in golf is—don't lose your sense of humor. Nobody survives the game without the ability to laugh at himself. (Or, herself—thank you, Dolores.) The game is literally bent on monkeying with us. Great players have been known to appreciate this quality in different ways. Ben Hogan insulated himself. Tommy Bolt externalized everything in hot flashes of temper and humor. Colorful language notwithstanding, Palmer, Demaret and Trevino have shown that gentlemen can use humor, even biting humor, on the golf course to make it a more enjoyable experience.

Golf in the Comic Strips uses the perceptive minds of the world's foremost cartoonists to capture the wild and woolly, the mysterious and rewarding allure of golf—what it does to its players and what it leaves them in return. Each strip is unique and will leave the golfer and the non-golfer with an extra appreciation for the game, as well as some howls of laughter at the folly of it all.

Who can fully explain the golfer's obsession with the game? Blistering sun, driving rain, sleet, snow and threatened marriages—we keep our eyes on that little white ball in hopes of a personal best, and we keep coming back for more. You gotta love the game. You gotta love this book.

Drawing by Jerry Dowling

INTRODUCTION

In the mid-1890s, a new art form began to emerge. It was spearheaded by artists like Richard F. Outcault, James Swinnerton and Rudolph Dirks, and two publishers, Joseph Pulitzer and William Randolph Hearst. This new art form would become known as the comic strip. At the same time, another craze was also capturing the eye of the country. It was an import from the shores of Scotland and was known as golf. In one of his earliest works, Outcault, then working for Hearst on the *New York Journal American*, did a series of panels with dialogue titled *The Yellow Kid Takes a Hand at Golf*.

When the Yellow Kid took his glorious swing in the last panel of that work, he was to inaugurate a remarkable 100-year relationship between golf and the comic strips. No other subject has been more parodied, satirized or used as a setting than golf. In the 14 years that I have been collecting from the pages of American newspapers what I now call GOLFTOONS®, I have assembled over 4,000 comic strips and cartoons on golf. Nearly every cartoonist who put pen to paper has found the subject of golf to be inspirational whether it be to express joy or sarcasm.

Golf had just been introduced to the United States in the early 1890s. Its rise in popularity was stunning among women as well as men. It can be assumed that most of the successful cartoonists of the day belonged to country clubs and the ability of golf to flummox the most agile athlete was not lost on them. After all, golf demands that you begin by smashing the pill, as it was then called, several hundred yards down the fairway and then finish by tapping it toward a small hole with the delicacy of a brain surgeon. Doing this for four to five hours tends to shred the nerves. It also teaches one to laugh at one's ineptitude and that provided fodder for the cartoonist's fertile imagination.

Here in America the comic strip has struggled to gain its rightful position in the ranks of American art. Renowned collector and curator of the *San Francisco Museum of Comic Art* Bill Blackbeard credits this to the fact that comic strips were the staple of the yellow journals, those papers that resorted to sensationalism to gain readership. They were considered low-brow. To this day, *The New York Times* does not carry comic strips. Around the world, however, this is not the case—especially in France and Japan where the American comic strip is deemed fine art. In the last few years there has begun an effort to preserve comic art. Mort Walker, of *Beetle Bailey* fame, spearheaded the construction of a $20 million museum in Boca Raton, Florida, and the Ohio State University, because of the efforts of Lucy Caswell, has a department dedicated to comic strip art. Bill Blackbeard's *San Francisco Museum of Comic Art* has tens of thousands of comic strip tear sheets dating back to the Yellow Kid as well as a vast library on the subject. The United States Post Office has just honored the comic strip with a 25-sheet commemorative issue.

The nature of the comic strip endows it with special powers. A comic strip has no limitations from time or space or decorum. In short, anything goes in the comics. Its protagonist can be a handsome hero in a skin-tight costume or a wisecracking cat, a goofy rubbernecked lady or a pinheaded clown or even a fluffy cloud making commentary about the actions of the humans below. The comic strip is like a short film. It has a location, performers and dialogue and it progresses through time. Each strip tells a little story. It reflects the culture of its times. As the reader pages through this book, he or she will get a sense of what not only golf was like, but what the country was like in each era.

This book is the result of my research efforts and my excitement for the story of golf and comic strips. There have been several books that have compiled collections of comic strips but this book is unique in the fact that all the strips are about golf. Recently I had the pleasure of playing golf with an old gentleman possessing a beautiful but not-too-powerful swing. At about the 16th hole, I found out he was 79 years old. I asked him if he used to read *The Gumps*. "No," he responded, "I never followed the comic strips closely." I told him that some of the best commentary ever done on golf was to be found in *The Gumps*. "Well, if I had known that I would have read them," he retorted.

I have included over 200 works in this book from more than 100 different artists. When deciding what strips to include, I considered humor, uniqueness, historical and political content, personalities and artistic style. The material is presented in a general historical progression.

I have included a smattering of exposition and commentary throughout the book to educate the reader about the artist or the period under consideration or the rationale for assembling certain strips together on a single page. But the stars of this book are the comic strips and for the most part I have let them speak for themselves. I have given many strips and cartoons a single page because I want the reader to be able to assimilate the power or the beauty of the work.

I would like to thank all the wonderful cartoon artists whose artistic creations have contributed mightily to the game of golf and I would like to apologize to those artists I was not able, for space reasons, to include.

For all of those who know they will never break par; who know they will never win any meaningful tournament but can't wait to get out on the links at 6 A.M. on Saturday morning; for all of those who see golf as an island of sanity in a hostile world, a garden of Eden on 150 acres of manicured terrain—it is for them that the comic strip speaks and to whom I dedicate this book.

GEORGE WASHINGTON IS DECLARED TO HAVE BEEN A LOVER OF MANY KINDS OF OUTDOOR SPORTS

BY MYER

1901

THE YELLOW KID TAKES A HAND AT GOLF.

TEEING
OFF

THE YELLOW
KID TAKES A
HAND AT
GOLF

BY RICHARD F.
OUTCAULT

1897

On October 24, 1897, *The Yellow Kid Takes a Hand at Golf* appeared in the American Humorist supplement of *The New York Journal,* a paper owned by William Randolph Hearst. Only a few months earlier, Richard Outcault, an American born in 1863 in Lancaster, Ohio, had invented a distinctive new art form soon to be known as the comic strip.

In 1895, Outcault had made a name for himself by drawing a series of cartoons that appeared in *The New York World*, a paper owned by Joseph Pulitzer. They featured the children of Hogan's Alley located in New York's Hell's Kitchen, an infamous immigrant ghetto. As the cartoons appeared each week, Outcault slowly developed a bald-headed, big-eared, nightshirted urchin who was to become known as the Yellow Kid. Amazingly, the first edition of *Hogan's Alley* in which the Yellow Kid had become clearly defined was titled *Golf—The Great Society Sport as Played in Hogan's Alley*. The Yellow Kid was a sensation, as big as *Peanuts* is today.

The glorious swing taken by the Yellow Kid, whose name was Mickey Dugan, was to begin a relationship between golf and the comic strips that has not waned in 100 years. It's noteworthy that the Yellow Kid's golfing form is quite exceptional. He uses a baseball grip but his swing in frame six shows great rhythm and full extention with his head remaining behind the ball. I doubt seriously if many Americans in 1897 could match his form!

LINK(S)ED SWEETNESS

1899

LUNATICS I HAVE MET

BY RUBE GOLDBERG

1907

LINK(S)ED SWEETNESS.

The Real Caddie (audibly) ___ "This club is going to ruin___allowing all these ladies to join!"
Miss Sharp___" They evidently can't get gentlemen!"____Punch's Almanack

Before the newspaper comic strip, Americans got their humor from magazines such as *Punch*, *Life*, *Judge* and *Truth*. From these magazines, newspapers often purchased reprint rights to cartoons such as *Link(s)ed Sweetness* which ran in *The Chicago Tribune* in 1899. As the magazines, which were relatively expensive, catered to the rich, the drawing was on the conservative side. In stark contrast was the loose style of *Lunatics I Have Met* by Rube Goldberg, which was much more akin to the tastes of the lower classes who were likely to read the newspapers.

In *Link(s)ed Sweetness* we see that women were as enamored by the new sport of golf as men. By 1900 there were several "ladies only" golf courses; including a nine-hole course at Shinnecock. The first gold medal won by any American in the modern Olympics was the one Margret Abbot won for golf in the 1900 Paris Olympics.

Rube Goldberg was probably the first cartoonist to recognize what fun could be had by exaggerating the contortions that one sees while observing golf. He was to become one of the most respected cartoonists in the country and is still known for his "Rube Goldberg Contraptions." He designed the Reuben, the annual award given to the year's outstanding cartoonists. Goldberg was an avid golfer and even wrote articles on the subject.

LOON XVIII
THE GOLF NUT.

MR ANANIAS STILL FINDS LIFE A BURDEN

WITHOUT HIS WIFE

This strip is one of the earliest documentations of the creation of the golf widow. Ananias is a biblical term meaning liar, and men, then and now, were willing to tell a small fib to steal away to the links.

Buster Brown (pages 14 and 15) was the most enduring creation of Richard Outcault, the inventor of the comic strip. The strip and the name Buster Brown were to become enormously famous and everything from shoes to bubble gum would exploit the name. The mischievous child was a prevalent theme in early American comic strips and Buster's imagination made him one of the best. The explosive power of a golf club hitting a ball was an infatuating force even in the early 1900s.

Mama's Angel Child demonstrates that little girls are as inquisitive—and naughty—as little boys. Angel Child's golf swing results in a beautiful finish demonstrating a good knowledge of golf by Ross. Penny Ross, a man, was an assistant to Outcault, and often helped with the drawing of *Buster Brown*.

The Wisconsin-born Briggs produced over 500 strips on golf, many of them classic in their perspective and insight. He is credited with being the originator of the first strip to run on a daily basis, *A Piker's Clerk*, which gave horse racing tips. His style was notable for its sentimentality and warmth and defense of the little man on the golf course.

James Swinnerton was born in Eureka, California. The son of a judge, he went, at 16, to work in San Francisco and was soon hired by William Randolph Hearst on his first paper, *The San Francisco Examiner*. There, he created a precursor to the comic strip called *Little Bears*, an amusing panel story without dialogue. His talent was exceptional and he soon was also doing full-page editorial cartoons. By the age of 21, he was a successful man. Hearst brought him to New York where he developed several comic strips, the most famous being *Jimmy*. Swinnerton's characters all had cute little bug eyes. This strip is quite notable for its ethnic dialogue, a reflection of the large number of immigrants who had come to America in the early 1900s.

Swinnerton contracted tuberculosis and moved to Arizona where he became world-renowned for his fine Southwestern oil masterpieces. He lived well into his 90s and hopefully he was able to play golf at some of the great courses in Arizona.

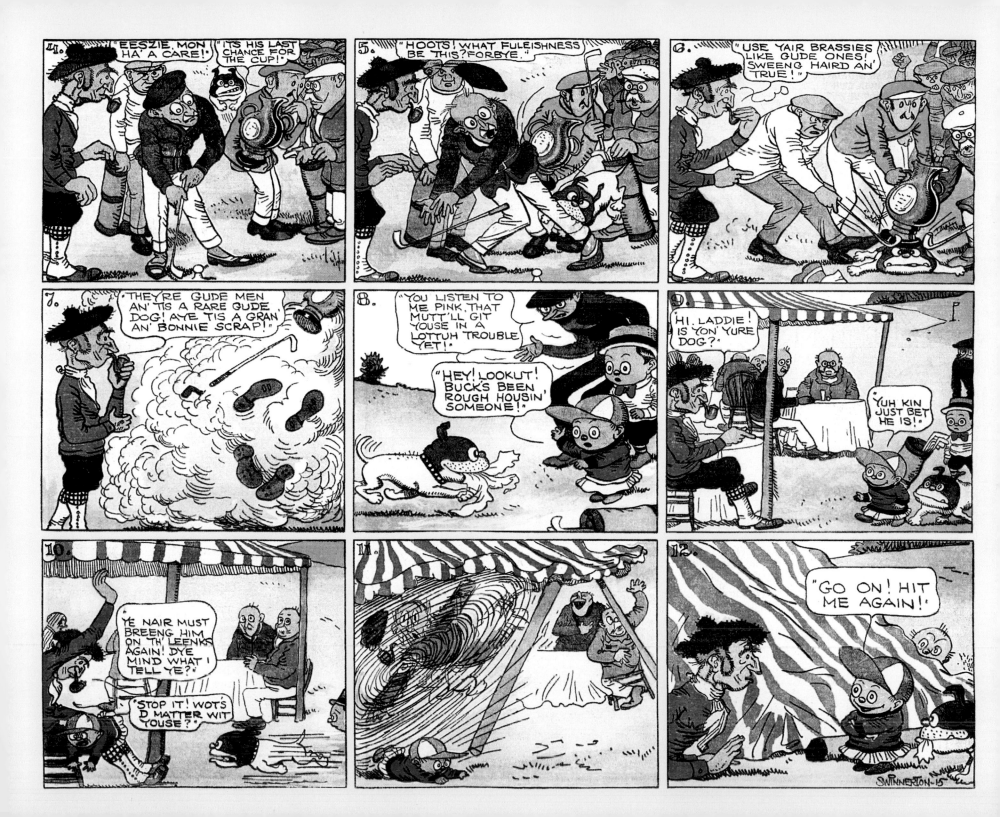

HARRY VARDON AND REID TIE

British Experts Lead in First
Half of Open Journey.

EACH GETS A CARD OF 147.

Edward Ray and H. Strong Land Near
Top with Scores of 149.

Brookline, Mass., Sept. 18 — Playing golf
of a caliber seldom seen in America, two of
the trio of English professionals forged to the
front today in the first half of the nineteenth
annual open tournament of the United States
Golf association and at dusk led the field by a
margin of two strokes.

Harry Vardon and Wilfrid Reid turned in
cards of 147 for the first thirty-six holes.
Edward Ray divided second place with
Herbert Strong of the Inwood club of Inwood,
N. Y., each having 149. MacDonald Smith of
New

Qualifying Scores in Golf Tournament.

	A.M.	P.M.	Tot.
Harry Vardon, England	75	72	147
W. E. Reid, England	75	72	147
Edward Ray, England	75	72	147
Herbert Strong, Inwood	79	70	149
MacDonald Smith, Wykagyl, N. Y.	75	74	149
J. M. Barnes, Tacoma, Wash.	71	79	150
W. Hagen, Rochester, N. Y.	74	76	150
Alex Ross, Bran Burn, Mass.	73	78	151
*Francis Ouimet, Woodland, Mass.	71	80	151
George Sargent, Chevy Chase, Md.	77	74	151
C. Thoto, Shinnecock, N. Y.	75	76	151
	76	76	152

WHEN A FELLER NEEDS A FRIEND

BY BRIGGS

1913

When a Feller Needs a Friend was a recurring theme explored by Briggs covering many topics other than golf. This strip, often called a panel strip, appeared in *The Chicago Daily Tribune* on the day after the first round of the 19th U.S. Open in Brookline, Massachusetts. The articles surrounding the strip are reports of the first day's results. This was, of course, the Open that was to be won for the first time by an American amateur, Francis Ouimet. Ouimet, a caddy at the Brookline club, was a virtual unknown and it is interesting to note not a word is mentioned about him in the article. In the qualifying scores on the bottom of the page he stands in ninth place. The powerful English contingent of Vardon, Reid and Ray holds the first three spots. On the final day Ouimet beat Vardon, known for his graceful rhythmical swing, and Ray, known for his 300-yard-plus drives, to win the championship. Briggs did *Ouimet* about a week after the tournament.

It is interesting to note that John McDermet was actually the first American to win the Open, a feat he accomplished as a teenager in 1911. As professionals were held in such low regard at that time—they were not considered to be gentlemen—little fanfare was accorded to McDermet.

Sidney Smith, like Briggs, began as a sports cartoonist. For many years he drew material critiquing the Chicago Cubs. Every once in a while he would sneak a strip in about golf, such as the one we see here. Later, Sidney Smith would go on to become the first comic strip artist with a million-dollar contract, for doing *The Gumps*.

In the first panel, the character in the strip refers to Joe Le Duc, a professional golfer known for his long drives.

Old Opie Dilldock appeared weekly in *The Chicago Tribune* beginning in 1906. Howarth had long been a respected cartoonist; his work often appeared in *Judge*. The strip was always about some convoluted fantasy accented with hyperbole. The title should be pronounced OL–DOPIE DILLDOCK.

A GOLF YARN IN THE MAKING
BY SIDNEY SMITH
1915

Reprinted by permission of Tribune Media Service.

OLD OPIE DILLDOCK'S STORIES.

I once played golf on horseback, just for novelty. Having 41,144 yards to make, I placed nine balls in a row, then galloped up, swung my driver, hit the first ball and that started the other eight in rotation.

I galloped after them full speed to catch any ball that might drop. One ball was falling in the bunker, but I swung the iron on it and drove it out of danger. Then I fled helter skelter after the rest.

Soon I came upon a ball that had fallen in the rough. It was buried deep, but I got out my niblick as I went flashing on and made a stroke at the ball. I dug up considerable earth and a bale of grass, but I made the shot.

With my driver in one hand and the iron in the other, I rushed on. Several of the balls were losing speed, so I touched 'em up a bit. Three of them got away from me, however, and fell in the sand pit. Hurriedly I took out my mashie.

With the mashie and niblick I entered the pit. One swing with each club was sufficient to lift the three runaway balls out of the sand. I tapped them lightly, for I was almost upon the green.

All the balls were lying on the edge of the green. I got beneath the horse, going full gait, and with my putter tapped the balls into the hole. They wouldn't all go in, of course, so I putted them one on top of the other in a spiral. Frank Presbrey never would believe it could be done.

Old Doc Yak was the first doctor to play golf in the comics. Sidney Smith's creation ran from the early 1900s to the 1930s. *Doc Yak* was one of the first anthropomorphic comic strip characters, showing how comics, by giving animals human characteristics, allowed the artist to take perspectives that would be otherwise impossible.

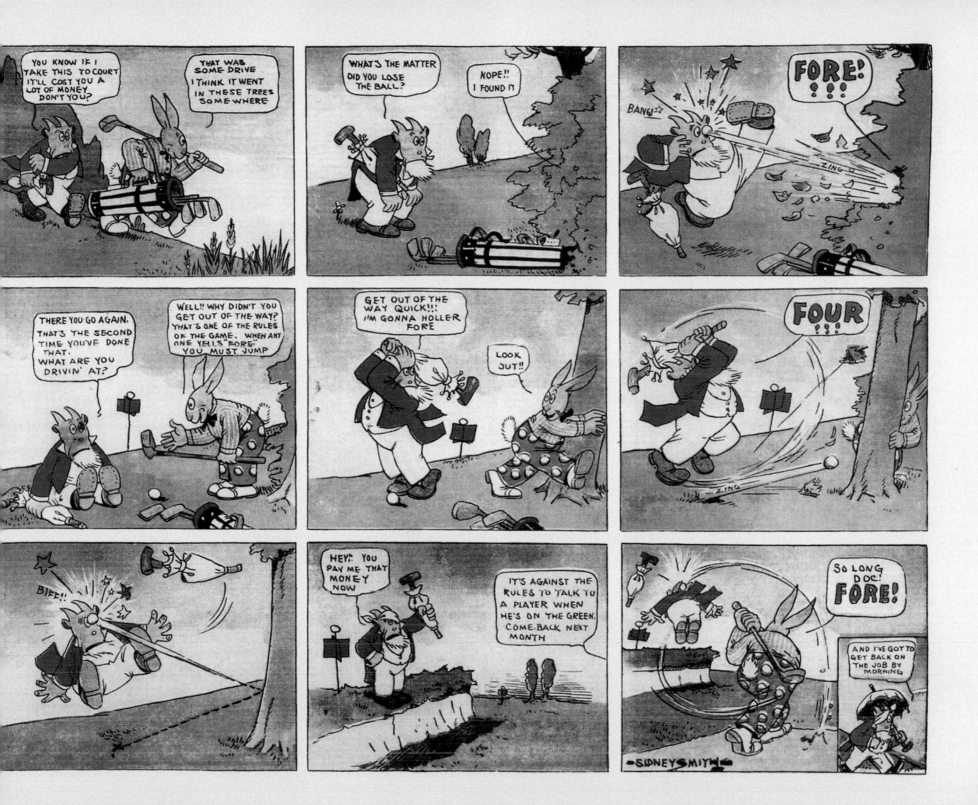

I love the fall the best of all
The seasons of the year
For when I dub or bust a club
There's not a person near

The *Beauty of Autumn Golf* and *Characters You'd Meet on Any Golf Course* show the diverse styles incorporated by Briggs to reflect upon nature and humanity as it pertains to golf.

By 1920 the daily strip had been firmly established. Strips such as Fisher's *Mutt & Jeff*, McManus's *Bringing Up Father*, Voight's *Poor Little Petey* and Willard's *Moon Mullins* (pages 28-29)showed that golf was now popular with the common people or "lowlifes," as they were sometimes referred to. The humor was often base and no group or individual was spared from being the butt of a joke. Public golf courses were on the rise and the game was now available to almost everyone. Blacks were, for the most part, still confined to being caddies but even that experience had to give many of them a taste for the game.

    In *Mutt & Jeff*, Jeff caddies for President Harding, who usually had trouble breaking 100.

MOON MULLINS

BY FRANK WILLARD

1928

Men may have thought that the golf course was their own private domain, but women have had things their own way from the start—although most men don't know it. In *And Getting Paid For It*, the caddy happily carries the lady's bag whereas in *Pantomime*, the lady proudly struts down the center of the fairway while the men spread to the far reaches of the rough. In *Deb Days* we see that even a pro is no match for a lady.

C. J. Coll

THE GOLF CHAMPION MISSES HIS PUTT

Eve is watching a golf tournament at a country club where a handsome young golf champion is playing a final match. Eve has been following his brilliant career, and at this moment she is doing some silent and concentrated hero-worshiping as he sets his lean, firm jaw and broad shoulders for a drive. With a clear, sharp click, he hits the ball, sending it over treetops and the brook, directly toward the green for more than 250 yards. The crowd follows the players, while the champion gains, falls behind, and at the eighteenth hole needs only to make a simple two-yard putt to win the close and exciting match.

Eve's eyes are glowing and her cheeks are flushed for she has been mentally playing every stroke and concentrating on her hero winning the match.

As he walks across the green to make his final putt, his eyes are arrested by a vivid spot. It is Eve, with her gold hair shining in the sun, her eyes sparkling, her red lips parted. She is wearing a gay green sports frock and a green hat, beneath which her eyes look into the champion's with a rapt gaze.

After a long moment, the crowd waiting—he bends over his ball ready to putt. He waits, changes his stance—waits—then hits the ball, sending it a foot wide of the hole. The crowd groans with disappointment: They cannot understand it. All around are murmurs of "a cinch" — "nothing to it" — "why" — "how did he do it!"

A few weeks later, the golf champion meets Eve at a dinner party and lets her in on his dark secret of why he missed the foolish putt. Eve's loveliness, he tells her, was so disconcerting that it knocked him "for a row of lilies!"

Reprinted by permission of The Tribune Media Service.

THE TINY TRIBUNE

BY ORR

1918, 1919

World War I put the breaks on America's infatuation with golf but by no means did it bring it to a standstill. Only cartoonists could combine golf and war. *The Tiny Tribune* by Orr is a compilation of four different strips featuring only the sections on golf. Briggs did many strips on the war including one that always ended with "Damn the Kaiser"—referring to how the war was interfering with golf.

The tin-hatted *Happy Hooligan* was one of the most beloved comic strip characters of all time. He was the creation of Frederick Opper, whose career began at the age of 14 when he went to work at a paper in his hometown of Madison, Ohio. *Happy Hooligan* ran from 1900 to 1932 and was always optimistic and willing to try anything, including golf.

A GOLFER IS A NATURALLY TRAINED SOLDIER

BY BRIGGS

1917

The shenanigans and traumas of the country club were fecund ground for the imagination of the cartoonist. *In the Rough*, although short-lived, was a strip devoted completely to golf. Voight, who went on to do *Betty*, did many strips on golf. Jack Lustig, a sports cartoonist for the *San Francisco Examiner*, enjoyed poking fun at the bickering at the country club.

"Who's that stranger Mother, dear? Look! he knows us Aint he queer?"

"Hush my own don't talk so wild; he's your Father, dearest child"

"He's my father? No such thing; Father died away last Spring"

"Father didnt die, you dub, Father joined a golfing club"

"But they closed the club so he Has no place to go, you see"

"No place left for him to roam That is why he is coming home"

"Kiss him........he won't bite you child- All them golfing guys look wild.

The pictures are ours- -Loud cries of Author-Author"

ALAS! WHAT A SAD SIGHT IS THIS! THE UNHAPPY CREATURE HAS JUST DISCOVERED, TOO LATE, HER HUSBAND IS A SLAVE TO GOLF AND IS EVEN NOW, ERE SHE HAS REMOVED HER WEDDING GARMENTS, ON HIS WAY TO THE LINKS TO JOIN ROISTERING COMPANIONS..... SUCH SCENES AS THIS MAY BE AVOIDED IF ONLY YOUNG GIRLS WOULD HEED THE COUNSEL OF THEIR ELDERS AND BEWARE OF HASTY MARRIAGES.

THE GOLF ECONOMIST

BY KESSLER

1923

Losing a ball was an expensive error as we see in Frank King's *Gasoline Alley*. As Kessler shows in *The Golf Economist*, repainting golf balls was a good chore to take care of during the winter. But Fontaine Fox, with his delightful country humor learned in his hometown of Louisville, Kentucky, shows that breaking a club was an option irrespective of cost.

THE TERRIBLE TEMPERED MR. BANG

BY FONTAINE FOX 1924

THE MYSTERIOUS STRANGER
BY JOHN MCCUTCHEON
1925

Alcohol, for better or for worse, has always been associated with golf. In fact, the bar in the clubhouse, as every golfer knows, is known affectionately as the 19th hole. McCutcheon was the front-page editorial cartoonist for *The Chicago Tribune* for many years but even in that capacity he managed to use golf from time to time to make a point or, in this case, warn golfers in the clubhouse to be on the alert. This cartoon was drawn during prohibition and it was no secret that there was plenty of booze at the country club.

Pops (page 42) was one of the few British imports to be successful on the American comic page. Its dry cogent humor got right to the point. *Lord Chumpleigh* never gained large popularity but its clean lines and style had a definite charm.

It is rumored that Dry Agents, disguised as golf players, may visit the locker rooms.

Rudolph Dirks began working for William Randolph Hearst on *The New York Journal* around 1898. He was given the task of creating a mischievous child strip based on two characters in a German cartoon called *Max und Moritz*. The result was the *Katzenjammer Kids*, one of the most delightful strips in comic strip history. The ethnicity of the dialogue

44

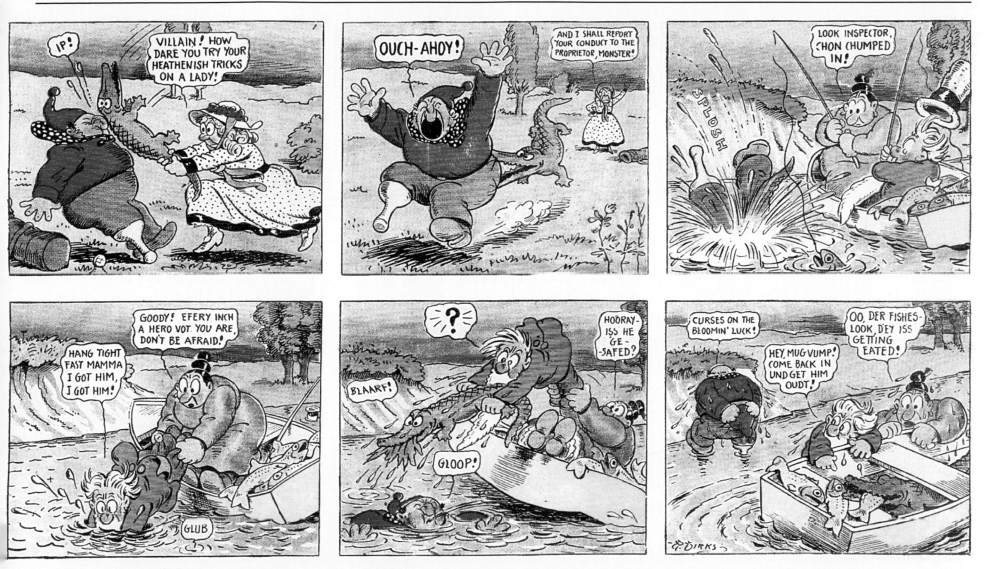

is one of the most charming aspects of the strip. Dirks was one of the true innovators in comic strips. Conventions such as speed lines and sweat drops came from his brilliant mind. Over time the strip was renamed *Hans and Fritz* and then *The Captain and the Kids*. Golf was a special experience in the world of *Hans and Fritz*—a frightening experience.

THE GIRL STRIP

During the '20s, what was known as the "girl strip" was a popular format with cartoonists. Some of these strips might be called sexist now or degrading to women, but in reality they portrayed men and women in much the same way. In *Beautiful Babs*, we find Oliver, the male, portrayed as an athletic and mental incompetent and in *Dulcy, the Beautiful Dumbbell* the role is reversed. What is important is that they were all playing golf!

Beautiful Babs is done by Murat Young, who changed his name to Chic Young and went on to create the most popular family strip of all time: *Blondie*.

School Days was done by Clare Victor Dwiggins, a native of Ohio. The strip appeared daily as a panel and as a color strip on Sunday. Poor kids played a game called "shinny" in which they would hit a can with makeshift golf sticks. Real golf was way beyond the meager finances of the poor but a little imagination could overcome a lot of obstacles.

THE PEST
BY BRIGGS
1924

A GREAT DEAL CAN BE DONE
WITH THE IMAGINATION
BY BRIGGS
1918

Each year Clare Briggs would do a series of panel strips that would encompass the feelings of dismay that the onslaught of winter brings to golfers, the frustation of not being able to play golf for several months and the joy of hitting the links on the first day of spring. Here we see a mix of some of the best of those works that appeared over a decade.

By 1929 it was apparent that golf was here to stay and Moran, a sports cartoonist, has a little laugh by poking fun at the snobs who thought it was just a passing fancy.

The idea for *Joe Palooka* (page 52) came from the inspiration of a dumb but talented prizefighting friend of Ham Fisher. Joe Palooka was a product of the depression. His good looks, innocence and fortitude were inspirational to Americans struggling to survive in their daily lives.

The two strips shown here herald the esteem that the country held for Bobby Jones. In a prior strip Bobby had been in attendance at Joe's last fight and a friendship ensued. Many boxers have been avid golfers, notably Joe Louis and, most recently, Oscar De La Hoya.

DID YOU SAY "GOOD OLD DAYS"?

BY MORAN

1929

THE GUMPS/HOME, JAMES   BY SIDNEY SMITH   1925

The Gumps was the first successful continuing strip, the story running day to day. The loyalty of its followers is legendary.

In the mid-'20s, Sidney Smith did this series of strips on golf that are truly unique. The dialogue in these works combined satire, hyperbole and metaphors to produce a remarkable and adorable statement about our beloved game.

In 1935, after celebrating a lucrative contract extention, Smith sped back late at night to his estate in Conneticut. He was killed in a head-on car crash. The strip continued under different artists for many decades.

THE GUMPS/THE $ A MINUTE MAN BY SIDNEY SMITH 1926

THE GUMPS/GOLF SLANGUAGE   BY SIDNEY SMITH   1926

A slapstick adventure strip, molded after Sherlock Holmes, *Hawkshaw the Detective* appeared in 1913. It was the creation of Charles Mager, who went to work for Hearst at the age of 20. Mager was a naturalist and fine artist, to which he devoted his entire time in his later years. His work has been collected by the Whitney Museum in New York as well as others.

It is quite amusing that diving for "lake-balls" is a practice that has a long history.

Cliff Sterrett, born in Freyers Falls, Minnesota, was one of the finest graphic artists to ever draw a comic strip. *Polly and Her Pals* ran for 46 years. Sterrett went to work for William Randolph Hearst at *The Journal American* in 1912 where he came up with a strip called *Positive Polly.* Later the name was changed to *Polly and Her Pals.* Polly was the first strip that featured a pretty society girl as its protagonist. She is

always shocking her parents, Maw and Paw, with her racy
outfits for which Sterrett took much heat from the censors.
Sterrett's style displayed daring and artistic imagination, each
panel being a piece of art.

Sterrett was known to enjoy a round of golf with his
cartoonist buddies.

MICKEY BRINGS GOLF TO HIS BARNYARD FRIENDS

MICKEY MOUSE

BY WALT DISNEY

ALL 1930

Walt Disney became famous in the '20s when he created the animated cartoon, *Steamboat Willie*, starring Mickey, a mouse who would soon become endeared around the world. Disney's animation led to his characters appearing in comic strips. The strips on these pages are from 1930 and show that Mickey and his barnyard friends have discovered how much fun golf is. The infectious smiles on the characters' faces and imaginative situations depicted in the strips easily explain why they became so popular.

Walt Disney played a bit of golf in his younger days and produced four cartoon shorts on the subject, but his primary sport was polo (golf on a horse?).

61

Fontaine Fox was born in Louisville and his delightful country humor reflects that fact. His drawing style had a unique and simple charm. Fox's many strips on golf covered different aspects of the game from a perspective that only his characters could offer. These characters, based on people he knew, were common working-class people and they reflected the fact that golf was no longer just a game for the elite classes.

Windy Riley by Ken Kling dealt with sports almost exclusively. Americans were very sports oriented in the '20s. It was the era that produced Babe Ruth and Bobby Jones. Windy is a hustler, a guy who will try anything to make a buck. The strips here are a sampling of a story that continued over a two-month period in *The San Francisco Chronicle*.

WINDY RILEY/WINDY MAKES A DATE   BY KEN KLING   1927

After Windy discovers he's a golf whiz, he enters a tournament being held at the Los Angeles Country Club. Windy makes a hole in one on the first tee and becomes an instant sensation. This leads him to become a professional and tour the country, during which a series of bizarre adventures occurs.

WINDY RILEY/A HOLE IN ONE   BY KEN KLING   1925

Ella Cinders began in 1925 and appeared as a Sunday strip in 1927. Set primarily in Hollywood, it was a twist on the classic fairy tale, *Cinderella*, and featured the lovely Ella Cinders and her evil stepmother. Her brother Blackie offered consolation and kindness

when needed. Bill Conselman wrote the text and Charlie Plumb created the drawings. In the episode depicted, Blackie, who is in military school, shows that golf can be educational in academic ways. Note the nice form displayed by the young man in the fourth frame.

GASOLINE ALLEY

BY FRANK KING

1936

These strips from *Gasoline Alley* are excerpts from a three-month series that ran in 1936. Doc has decided to play a golf ball across the country.

In the '20s stunts like this were not uncommon. If fact, in 1927, a plumber and golfer by the name of Joe Grahame set out to achieve the same goal. He disappeared somewhere in the middle of Texas.

Barney Google

Barney Google, created in 1919, was a sensational success when it appeared. The very talented Bill DeBeck built his strip using a race horse theme starring his wobbly kneed horse, Spark Plug. It was set in what could be called the low-life world and the vernacular was that of the street.

DeBeck was addicted to golf and was known to miss deadlines because of his excessive time on the links. This is born out by Barney's presidential campaign promise of "better golf courses and no green fees." DeBeck was well-liked and a fun person to be around. He often played golf with Dizzy Dean and Babe Ruth, as well as with his closest friend Frank Willard (*Moon Mullins*) and other cartoonists such as Rube Goldberg and Cliff Sterrett.

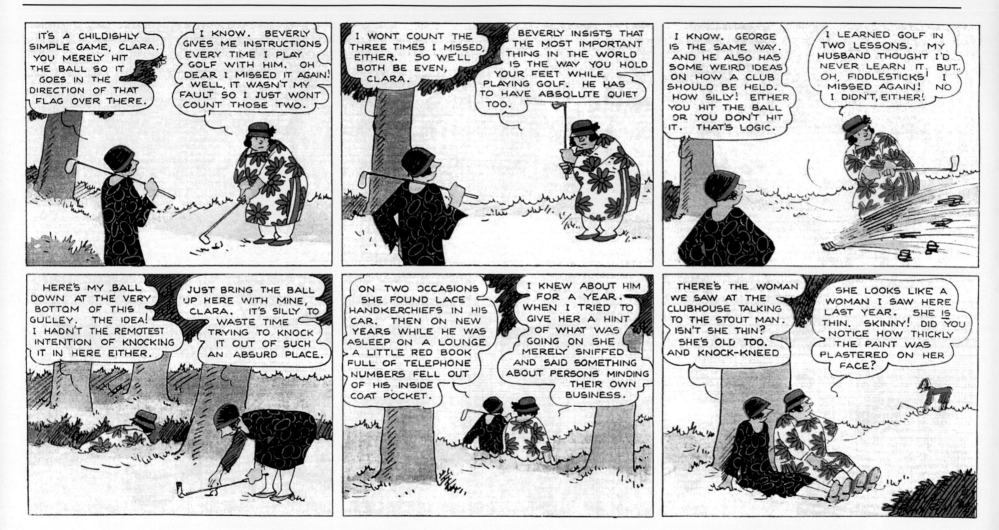

Harry Tuthill drew *The Bungle Family* for almost 20 years. Golf was used as a theme from time to time, usually in some sort of incredibly askew adventure. Tuthill's characters always outdid each other in their simplicity and audacity. George Tuthill was a bungler and in constant battle with his wife who was innocently naive. They probably gave many American families a chance to laugh at themselves. The Bungles became cult figures and many people were disappointed when the strip abruptly ended after Tuthill had an argument with his syndicator in 1939. Tuthill quit cartooning and lived his life out in his hometown of Ferguson, Missouri.

Little Folks was the '30s version of *Peanuts*. It was conceived by Captain Joseph Patterson, the great publisher of *The Chicago Tribune* who was the godfather of comics during the '20s and '30s, being responsible for *The Gumps*, *Dick Tracy* and *Smitty* just to name a few. Patterson was known for his ability to develop artists by giving them strip ideas that he conceived. *Little Folks* was not one of Patterson's successes and only lasted a couple of years but the teen dialogue in this strip is exceptionally cute.

Divot Diggers ran for over a decade in the Sunday comic section. It was the first successful strip devoted exclusively to golf, an indication of how popular the game had become. Vic Forsythe created several strips during the '20s, including *Joe Jinks* and *Fussy Foursomes*. He often played on the contrast between bigmouthed and insecure characters or the trials, tribulations and meanderings of the little man.

The '30s ushered in the adventure strip *Dick Tracy*, *Little Orphan Annie*, *Terry and the Pirates* and, of course, *Smilin' Jack* (pages 77 and 78). *Smilin' Jack* played on Mosley's detailed knowledge of aircraft and was one of the most popular strips of the day. In the episode depicted (pages 78 and 79), Jack finds a new use for the golf course.

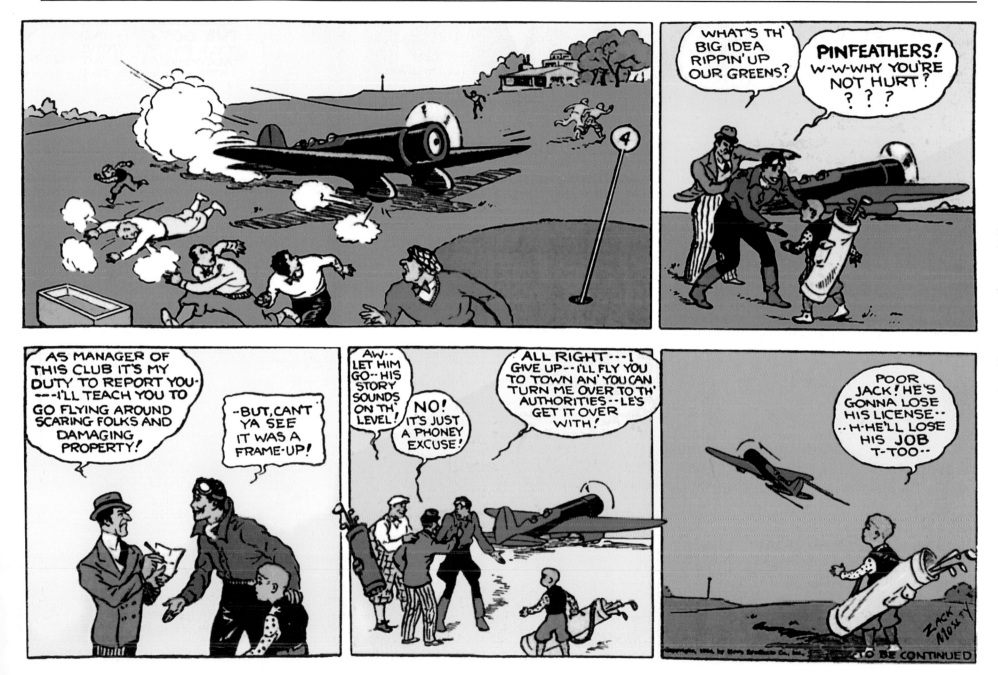

OH, MY GOODNESS! I'M NOT SUPPOSED TO HAVE MORE THAN FOURTEEN CLUBS! I'D BETTER THROW ONE AWAY BEFORE SOMEONE COMES ALONG AND CATCHES ME

MR. MILQUETOAST, PLAYING ALONE, REACHES THE 17TH HOLE BEFORE DISCOVERING THAT HE HAS 15 CLUBS —

The Timid Soul featured Mr. Milquetoast, a most timorous man. With all the overwhelming negativity facing the world at the beginning of World War II, it is no wonder that Americans related to this poor fellow. The word *milquetoast* has found its way into the English language and refers to a person lacking temerity.

Webster was the Briggs of the '30s. He dealt with the emotional foibles of the little man. He did many panel strips about golf, always showing a side to the game that dealt with the soul. On Sundays, *The Timid Soul* ran as a color comic strip. Webster has been called the Mark Twain of cartoonists.

As we have seen, little girls have loved to play golf since its introduction to America.

Kitty Higgins was done by Frank Willard. She was Kayo's playmate, Kayo being Moon's little urchin brother, and eventually she earned her own comic strip.

Little Lulu was the offering of a very successful female cartoonist, Marjorie Buell. Buell signed her strips as Marge. She modeled the character of Little Lulu after herself as a child. The character of Little Lulu became immensely popular and, as did most celebrities, took a hankering to golf.

Dudley Fisher's *Right Around Home* starred the ebullient Myrtle. She was modeled after Fisher's own teenage daughter. If Fisher's daughter had a swing like Myrtle's, she could have joined the women's tour.

KITTY HIGGINS

BY FRANK WILLARD

1932

LITTLE LULU

BY MARJORIE BUELL

1957

RIGHT AROUND HOME

BY DUDLEY FISHER

1944

The end of World War II brought some new innovations to the golf course. The advent of the pull cart would eliminate carrying the bag but on a sad note it spelled the end of the caddy. Mickey is a detective and his Uncle Phil, endowed with a good Irish temper, is also with the police department. Uncle Phil loves golf and despite his lousy scores always comes back for more. Lank Leonard drew a sports cartoon for 10 years for *The New York Sun* before doing the *Mickey Finn* strip.

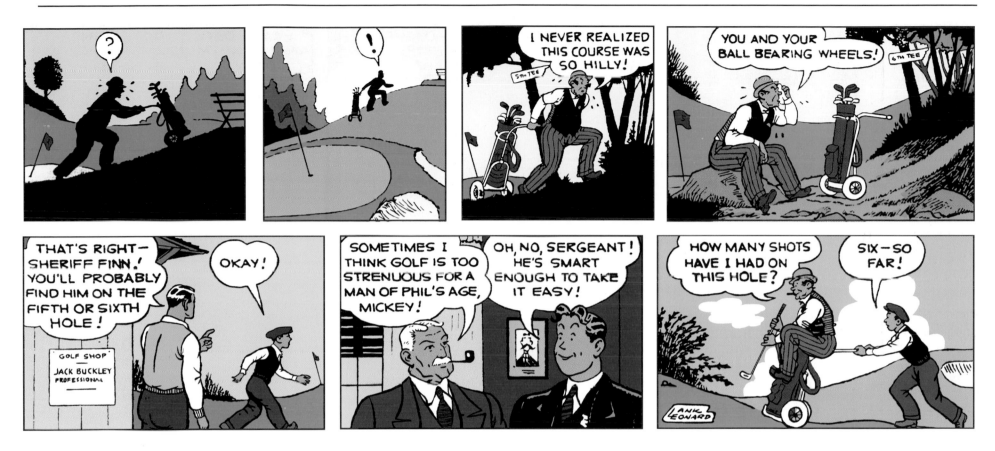

Abbie an' Slats (pages 84–97) first appeared in 1937. Van Buren had been a popular illustrator in *The Saturday Evening Post* and his artistic style gave the strip a sense of beauty as well as adventure. Van Buren was eventually inducted into the National Cartoonist Society's Hall of Fame.

The setting for *Abbie an' Slats* is Crabtree Corners. The strip is named for the young handsome Slats and his good-hearted Aunt Abbie, but many of the best stories revolve around the irascible Bathless Groggin, the father of Slat's girlfriend Becky. Only golf could inspire a story such as the one about to follow, which appeared over a seven-week period.

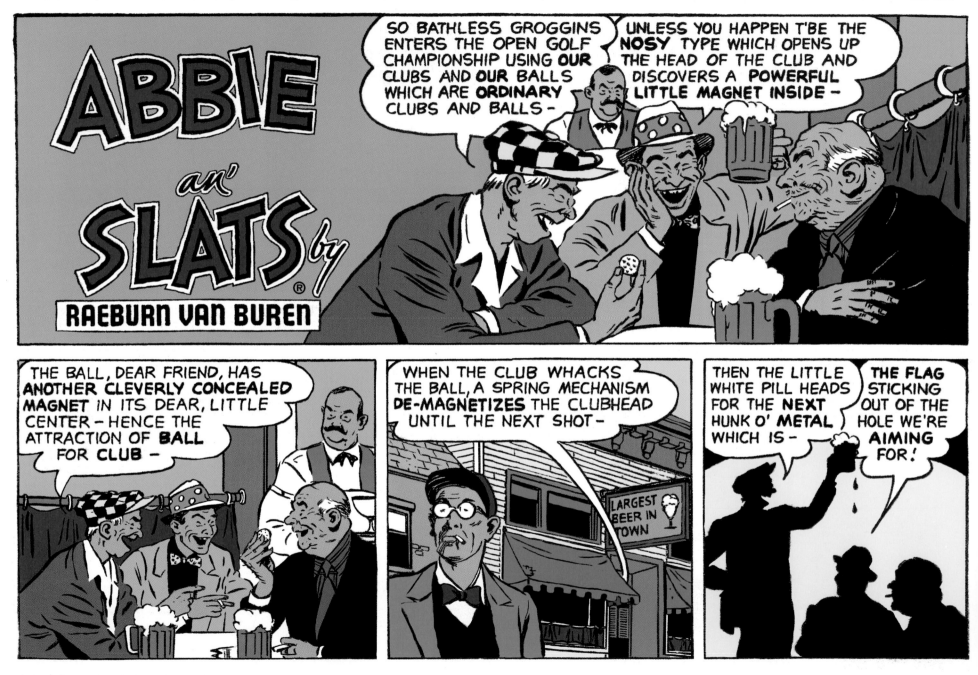

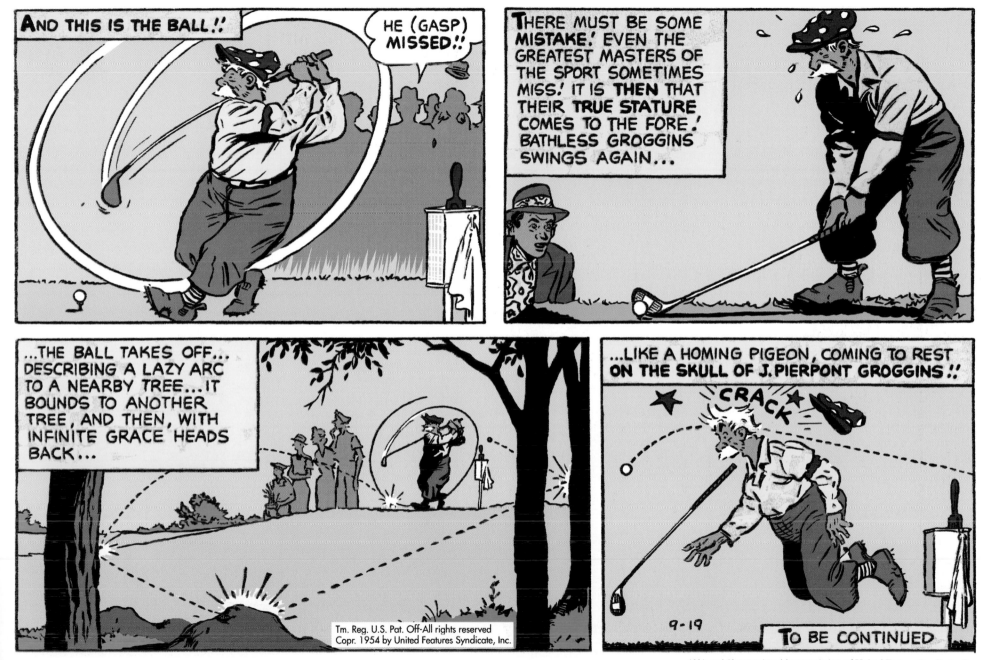

Abbie an' Slats reprinted by permission of United Feature Syndicate, Inc.

© Tribune Media Service, reprinted with permission.

© Tribune Media Service, reprinted with permission.

© Tribune Media Service, reprinted with permission.

ROMANCE ON

THE GOLF COURSE

HAROLD TEEN

BY CARL ED

1955

Harold Teen first appeared on the Sunday page in 1919. It was the first strip to deal with teenage life and its accompanying surge of hormones. This condition did not subside on the golf course. The strip became extremely popular during the '20s and ran for 50 years. *Harold Teen* introduced a whole new teenage vernacular to the world: profusely illustrated in the story shown.

The story line on these pages ran for nearly two months. Harold's friend, Shad, a soda lover above all, has gotten a job on the golf course as a caddy. When Teen discovers how gorgeous the pro's daughter is he wrangles his way into caddying for her. The episode ends when both Teen and Shad find out the pro's daughter is in love with a "hunk," which leaves them both out in the cold. Hey guys, take up golf!

Carl Ed taught at the Chicago Museum of Fine Arts, where he instructed many other cartoonists who would go on to fame.

One of the most lovable characters to appear in the *Joe Palooka* strip was Humphrey, a large powerful man with a heart as big as a house and a simple farm boy wisdom. In a broad comparison, Humphrey could be called the John Daly of his era.

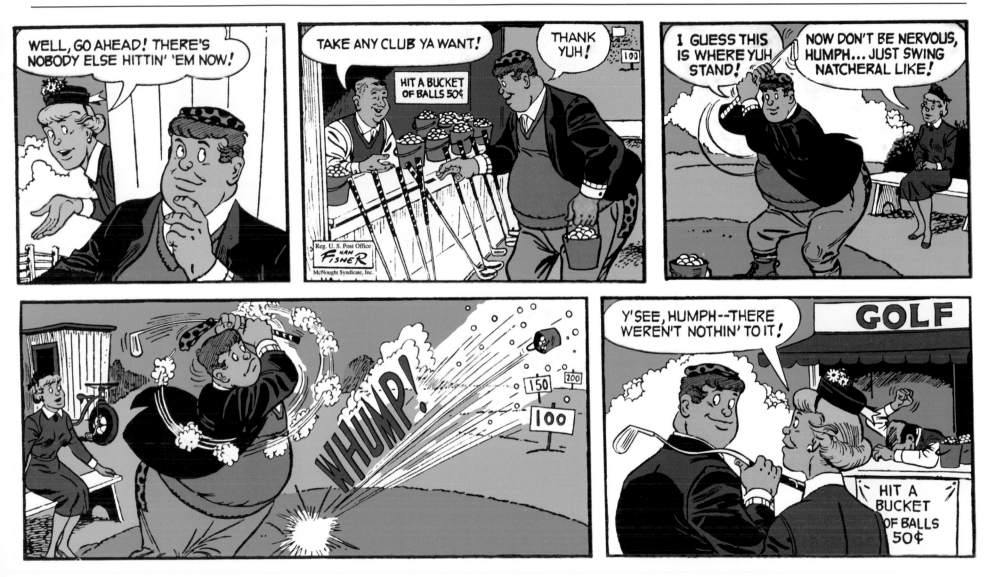

MACHINATIONS
IN PARADISE

STEVE ROPER
BY SAUNDERS
& OVERGARD
1962

© Tribune Media Service,
reprinted with persmission.

As television became the primary medium of America, it isn't surprising that comic strips would adapt formats similar to TV shows. In fact, John Saunders was a television producer and news anchorman before becoming a scripter for his *Steve Roper* comic strip. The strip still enjoys wide popularity today.

Steve Roper, a tough handsome detective, discovers that his putative golf date has more than breaking par in mind.

Originated in 1931 as a response to the gangster era, Chester Gould's *Dick Tracy* has been in publication ever since. Over the years, Tracy has been admired by the public for his relentless battle against grotesque and deranged criminals.

Golf plays a part in one of the few episodes in which the criminal is sympathetic. Could it be any other way? Mr. Pardee, a reformed criminal, hits an errant shot which unfortunately goes through a small hole in a broken pane of glass. The ball strikes the widowed woman living there, leaving her two children orphaned. The whole thing takes place in the middle of winter so there are no witnesses. Mr. Pardee is at a loss about what to do.

Reprinted with special permission of King Features Syndicate.

Little Iodine, which began appearing in 1943, was according to her creator, Jimmy Hatlo, the embodiment of every brat he knew. Her father, Henry Tremblechin, was always trying to impress his boss, Mr. Bigdome. Little Iodine was different from other cartoon kids in that she always seemed to know what was really going on.

Hatlo had worked for several papers, including *The Los Angeles Times* and *San Francisco Examiner*, as a sports cartoonist when in 1929 he came up with *They'll Do It Every Time*. King Features signed him and it became one of the most popular strips in America.

Mr. Mum's adventures seemed to bring him face to face with surrealistic events, even when he was trying to get in a game of golf. Phillips's strip was one of the first to use this technique, which may have been inspired by the new era of space travel that was upon the world.

Mort Walker is a lover of golf and has given tremendously to the sport through his creative comic strips. The *Beetle Bailey* strip, when introduced in the early '50s, was about a college kid called Spider, but soon took on its army theme. His most lovable character is General Halftrack, who I would suspect is autobiographical, at least when it comes to golf. Mort Walker is an excellent golfer, having shot as low as 68. He often jots down comic notes on his scorecard when inspired by some golfing mishap or absurdity.

THE STRANGE WORLD OF MR. MUM
BY PHILLIPS
1965

THE
MARRIED GOLFER

In the mid-20th century, a revolution took place in American family life. Women, who had made major contributions in the workplace during the war, were no longer content to sit at home doing their "wifely" chores. Equality was now the name of the game. This revolution was recorded in the comic strips with cogent clarity as it related to golf, on and off the course.

We'll be a close-knit family. We'll do everything together.

DONALD DUCK

BY WALT DISNEY

1959

Donald Duck is often seen playing golf and, as this strip shows, much to Daisy's chagrin.

The Lockhorns were created in 1968 by Bill Hoest. It won the National Cartoonist Society's best syndicated panel award in 1976 and again in 1980. Many of the Lockhorn's spats are over golf. Bill Hoest died in 1988 but the strip is continued by his wife, Bunny, and still features plenty of golf jokes.

THE LOCKHORNS

BY BILL HOEST

1984

NANCY

BY ERNIE BUSHMILLER

1960

Five great masters of the "kid strip"—Anderson, Bushmiller, Ketcham, Key and Keane—use the imagination, charm and enthusiasm of youth to remind us that golf brings out the child in all of us.

DENNIS THE MENACE

BY HANK KETCHAM

1959

"... An' he couldn't hit it, an' he couldn't hit it! So he said a bad word and KICKED it!"

HAZEL

BY TED KEY

1973

"Bad lie?"

THE FAMILY CIRCLE

BY BILL KEANE

1960

111

It can be argued that the White man took more from the Native American than he gave back, but for those Indians who have discovered the joy of golf, the trade may not have been that unfair. In this episode of *Rick O'Shay*, which ran for a month, the chief builds his own golf course on some swampland he owns. Business is slow until he announces gold has been found on the course. Of course, he's too savvy to let on

that the gold is just from his tooth. In the denouement, the chief makes a fortune out of his golf course by charging a fee to hunt for gold.

Stan Lynde was born in 1931 in Lodge Crass, Montana. While in the navy, he did a strip called *Ty Foon*, which gave him the cartooning bug. In 1958, he began *Rick O'Shay* for the Tribune News Syndicate.

Can Man and Woman
And Golf Coexist?

SMIDGENS
BY CORDRAY
1965

THE NEIGHBORS
BY GEORGE CLARK

THE BETTER
HALF
BY BOB BARNES
1965

*"I married him for better or worse,
and it didn't take me long to find out
which one it was."*

*"Did Shakespeare waste HIS time on the
golf course? I'll bet he was at HIS
typewriter all day long!"*

WOODY'S WORLD
BY WAP
1975

FRED BASSET
BY ALEXANDER
GRAHAM
1967

"What's that you say, Scout . . .
a 'people leg' to the right?"

MAC DIVOT

BY KEEFER & LANSKY

1957

Mac Divot was a daily serial strip about golf that ran for almost two decades. Mac Divot, a young handsome father figure, was all business on the course but always had time to console friends, relatives or fellow golfers in their time of need. Keefer and Lansky were from California. Lansky was a scratch golfer capable of breaking par and Keefer, who did the drawing, was happy breaking 100.

In the episode shown on these pages, Mac is fighting for the lead in the Hollywood Open.

The young caddies decide not to mention the broken club.

Mac, refusing to blame anyone, tries to overcome the handicap of being deprived of his driver. Against a strong wind he is unable to do so and loses the tournament by one stroke. When the young culprits come clean, Mac forgives them without a hint of animosity.

Reprinted with permission of Creators Syndicate, Inc.

TEENS

STRIPS

PENNY
BY DAHL
HAENIGSEN
1956

Throughout the 20th century, teenagers have defined American culture. Two wonderful examples of "goofy" teenage golf humor are *Archie* and *Penny*.

GIGS AND GAGS
BY CHET ADAMS
1948

"Well, I may be able to out-drive you, but I sure wish I had your short game!"

NUTS AND JOLTS
BY BILL HOLMAN
1948

"That's Ajax the butcher — he can't keep from slicing!"

TRIM'S ARENA
BY WAYNE STAYSKAL
1975

"Don't tell me . . . that was a slice, right?"

THE TREE TOP
COUNTRY CLUB

Shoe, the 1977 creation of three-time Pulitzer Prize winner Jeff MacNelly, is noted for its philosophical, sociological and psychological undertones. The MacNelly characters are Shoe, the Professor, his assistant Skyler, and Bumpkins. Their frequent forays to the treetop country club add a twist to golf humor and a bird's-eye perspective of the game. MacNelly, a large powerful man, also has won the Reuben Award twice. He claims he plays golf once a year, probably as inspiration for 5 or 10 great strips on why not to play the game.

1978

Frank and Ernest reprinted by permission of Newspaper Enterprise Association, Inc.

THE SPIRITUAL SIDE

OF THE GAME

Bob Thaves has won the Reuben Award three times for *Frank and Ernest*, a strip he created in 1972—and it's no wonder. Thaves is peerless when it comes to the cute quip. His scenarios take place anywhere, anytime and are always funny.

Thaves hails from Minnesota. After graduation, he became a consultant in industrial psychology. For a guy who doesn't consider golf his game (he's a racquetball player), he has given golf some of its most unique humor. He now resides in Manhattan Beach, California.

Frank is the taller character with the mustache.

If Friar Justin McCarthy, a man of the cloth, recognizes the spiritual side of golf, who are we to argue?

The vision of golf has never been the same since sports cartoonist Steve Moore put his spin on it. Moore mixes absurdity with reality to create something very special.

Art Sansom's Reuben Award–winning strip, *The Born Loser*, began in 1965. Sansom incorporates dry humor to make his witty and sarcastic points. Thornapple never gets away with anything, be it with his wife Gladys, his boss or his minister. Sansom always subdues little bursts of ego, which is why his humor is so appropriate for golf.

BROTHER JUNIPER
BY FR. JUSTIN McCARTHY AND LEN RENO
1963

"Here, here, none of that!"

"Whoa, bummer. Close, but no cigar. You don't get in . . . next!"

THE BORN LOSER
BY ART SANSOM
1987

WE MISSED YOU IN CHURCH THIS MORNING, BRO. THORNAPPLE!

GOLF AND POWER

By the mid-'60s, golf had become embroiled in the social issues of the day. Golf is now an established American right and is enjoyed by presidents and prisoners alike and, as we see in *Toppix*, caddies have rights, too. For those too young to remember, *Berry's World* refers to Richard Nixon returning from political oblivion to win the 1968 presidential election, the same year Arnie made his famous charge from 9 down to win the U.S. Open at Cherry Hills.

DUNAGIN'S PEOPLE

BY RALPH DUNAGIN

1980

6.5

"We know how that prisoner escaped from our minimum security facility . . . someone smuggled a hacksaw in with his golf clubs."

BERRY'S WORLD

BY JIM BERRY

1969

© 1969 by NEA, Inc.

"Mr. Palmer, this is the White House calling. The President would like to know if you would like to swap 'comeback' stories?"

TOPPIX

1976

CADDY POWER

THIS IS WHAT THE GAME IS ALL ABOUT!

5-2

YOU THE DOG!

The personae of two men has dominated golf for the last quarter century: Arnold Palmer and Jack Nicklaus. Arnie, as he was known to his army of followers, was famous for his charges on the final day and the awesome talent of Nicklaus was overwhelming to those who saw him play. One of Jack's fans, who followed him religiously around the country, began yelling "You the Man" whenever Jack hit a great shot. Much to Jack's chagrin, this accolade became a habit. Only one other golfer, as Schulz points out here, has earned the right to that enthusiastic cheer.

IT'S BIZARRE, HELEN. WHEREVER ARNIE GOES, THERE'S ALWAYS A SMALL ARMY OF NEIGHBORHOOD KIDS FOLLOWING HIM AROUND.

Arnold Palmer as a kid

IN THE BLEACHERS
BY STEVE MOORE
1993

Caricatures are a specialized offshoot of cartoon art. Two magazines, *Vanity Fair* and *The New Yorker*, are most responsible for the development of American caricature, an art form dating back to the early 1920s. Jerry Dowling, who won the Reuben Award for Best Newspaper Caricature Artist in 1994, has been drawing as long as he remembers. His teachers in high school often got quite upset with his renditions of them. Jerry was born in Canada but lives in Cincinnati, where he cartoons for the *Cincinnati Enquirer* and the Reds baseball team. He has also done a comic strip called *F-Stop Fitzgerald*. His best golf score is in the mid-70s but he's usually in the mid-80s or higher. Jerry is a realist and accepts his golf scores without rancor. As he has stated, "A cynic is an optimist with experience."

King's Island is in Cincinnati and, at the time this cartoon was drawn, was the home of the Nicklaus Golf Center. All the great lady pro's depicted had been winners at the yearly tournament held there.

127

One of the most controversial satirists of our times is Garry Trudeau. His strip, *Doonesbury*, began while he was at Yale and is noted for holding nothing sacred or sacrosanct and that includes golf.

*Sonny Bono—Rock and roll idol who performed with Cher. Went on to become mayor of Palm Springs, California, and then a U.S. Representative from California.

*George Hamilton—Playboy Hollywood actor. Married President Lyndon Johnson's daughter.

*Gerald Ford—33rd President of the United States and famous golfer. 12 handicapper, long off the tee but erratic when he plays in public tournaments.

129

Charles Schulz was a rail-thin kid from Minnesota who, as a youngster, played golf for his high school team. After serving in the army during World War II, he submitted an idea for a comic strip titled *Li'l Folks* to several publishers, only to have it thrown back at him with comments like "you can't draw." United Features picked the strip up in 1950 primarily because its square frames made it easy to use as filler in different sections of the paper. The editors at United Features renamed the strip *Peanuts*. Schulz hated the name but acquiesced. Peanuts delivered a laugh each day and is the most successful comic strip in history. Needless to add that Schulz has won every award conceivable.

B.C. first appeared in 1958. Hart began cartooning for the Pacific Stars and Stripes while serving with the Air Force in Korea. He submitted *B.C.* to five different publishers, being rejected by all until the *New York Herald Tribune* picked it up in 1958. *B.C.* is now in over 1,100 papers. Hart's incredible use of irony, double entendre, wit and satire have made his observations about golf unforgettable.

Lolly is Mr. Quimby's secretary and Mr. Quimby is an inveterate golfer, albeit a lousy one. *Lolly* is one of the few comic strips that features a secretary. Hansen has championed women's rights in many of his pieces.

The Born Loser reprinted by permission of Newspaper Enterprise Association, Inc.

THE WIZARD OF ID   BY PARKER & HART   1980

By permission of Johnny Hart and Creators Syndicate, Inc.

Bizarro ©1992 by Dan Piraro. Reprinted with permission of Universal Press Syndicate. All rights reserved.

BIZARRO
BY DAN PIRARO
1992

Dan Piraro is part of the new breed of cartoonist who mixes absurdity with realism and mysticism to make his point. After dropping out of art school, Dan bummed around Europe. Getting married forced him to settle down. Fellow workers at Neiman-Marcus encouraged him to submit his cartoons to syndicates. The result was *Bizarro*, which started running in 1985. Piraro has won awards for his oil paintings. His works on golf are always unique.

Tank McNamara is a sports strip that deals with hubris, disingenuousness and puerility in modern sports—especially as it relates to the professionals and the media. Millar & Hinds will often do strips on current golf topics such as African-Americans playing at Augusta or the image of the women's tour as presented by the media or the awesome difficulty of a particular course: "The bunkers are twenty-six feet deep, yes and the rough elephant grass, imported from Vietnam."

Tony Auth won the 1976 Pulitzer Prize for editorial cartoons, and needs only one word to express what is on the mind of every competitive golfer.

FULL DISCLOSURE
BY AUTH & SZEP
1982

Auth ©1982 The Philadelphia Inquirer. Reprinted with permission of Universal Press Syndicate. All rights reserved.

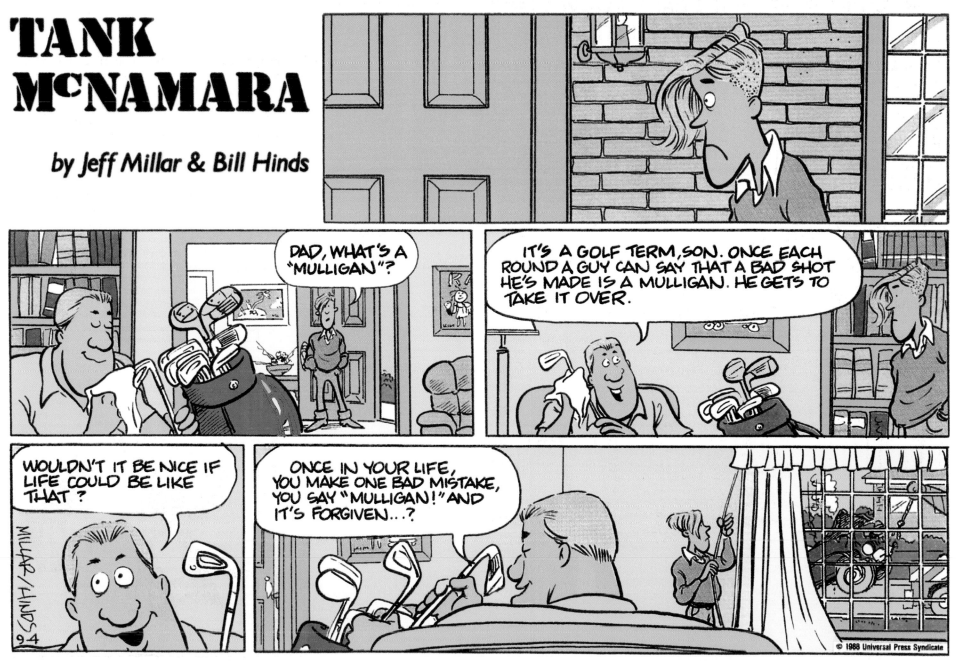

© Tribune Media Service. Reprinted with permission.

"I'll kick in my own locker,
if you don't mind!"

All cat lovers marvel at the stoic wisdom of those furry little creatures. *Basil*'s silent sarcasm, *Heathcliff*'s enthusiastic sarcasm and *Garfield*'s cynical sarcasm make their observations about golf something special. Only one dog has ever been able to match these feline philosophers, and that's the incomparable Snoopy.

HEATHCLIFF
BY GEORGE
GATELY
1978

A Brief Modern History
of Women and Golf

Since 1950, the role of women has taken a dramatic turn in society and, as would be expected, in golf. In *Nine to Five* the ladies are represented as pathetic weaklings. By 1970 this image was dispelled by Pete Hansen's Liz, a character in his strip *Lolly*. Then there was the lovable *Broom Hilda* who just knew how to be one of the boys. Finally, we have Nicole Hollander's *Sylvia*, which needs no added commentary. Nicole is from Chicago and has done everything from being a social worker to illustrating feminist periodicals.

NINE TO FIVE
BY JO FISHER
1950

"You're getting MUCH better distance—with those new balls. Hysteria . . . they go at least three feet."

LOLLY
BY PETE HANSEN
1973

Sylvia   by Nicole Hollander   1993

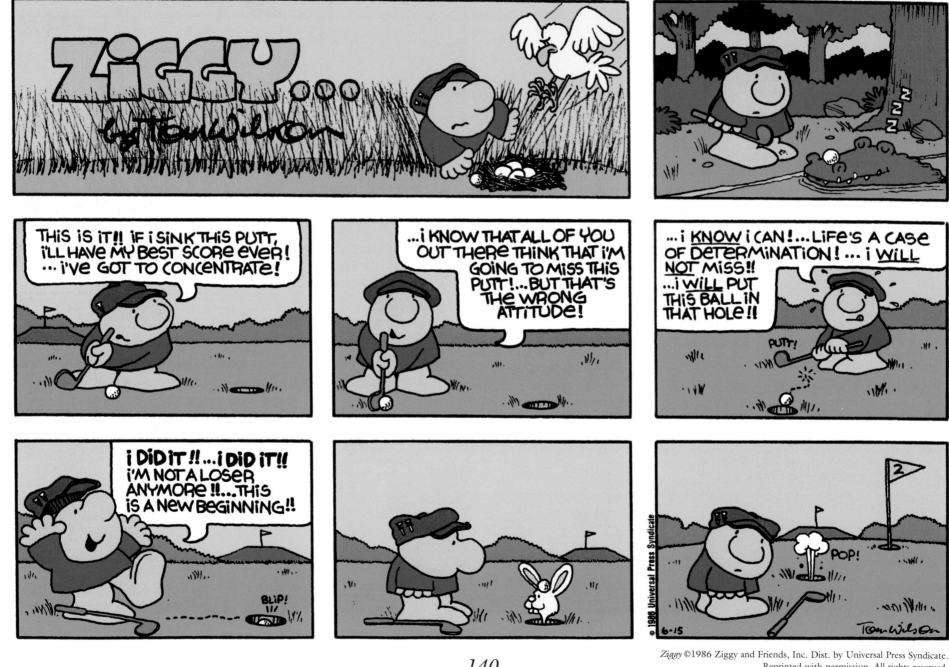

The amorphous *Ziggy* has been called America's most winning loser. Tom Wilson, a former greeting card artist, has created a character with whom anyone can identify. He has no race or color or ethnicity—he barely wears any clothes. But he is cuddly and cute and never walks off the golf course angry.

Bill Griffith and Don Addis suggest that golf may have nuclear capability. *Zippy* began as an underground comic strip but went mainstream after being picked up by King Features. Despite being a pinhead, Zippy has profound insights and is smart enough to get out on the golf course once in a while. Don Addis is a full-time editorial cartoonist for the *St. Petersburg Times*. He was born in Hollywood, which probably explains his penchant for the bizarre.

BENT OFFERINGS
BY DON ADDIS
1990

ZIPPY
BY BILL GRIFFITH
1991

141

Jump Start reprinted by permission of United Feature Syndicate, Inc.

HERB AND JAMAL
BY STEPHEN BENTLEY
1991

© Tribune Media Service,
reprinted with permission.

Two of the best African-American cartoonists, Robb Armstrong and Stephen Bentley, show us that golf has no racial boundaries. Bentley lives in Pasadena, California, and gets out when he can for a round at the many local courses. He based his strip on characters he knew in Los Angeles as a boy. In *Jump Start*, Armstrong makes the point that Michael Jordon has inspired black kids to take up the game, but with the age of Tiger Woods beginning, it is safe to assume that many more minority youngsters will want to know what the wonderful lure of golf is.

Blondie is one of the most widely circulated strips of all time. Created in 1930 by Chic Young, Blondie and her husband, Dagwood, have proven to be truly ageless. Over time, the characters of Blondie have adapted to the changing world. Like most family men, Dagwood plays golf, usually with his neighbor Herb or his boss, Mr. Dithers.

*D*ilbert has become the newest rage in the cartoon world. Conceived by Scott Adams, it focuses on life in the cubicles of corporate America, an environ that Adams was familiar with before creating his strip. Although the severe coldness of the cubicle world is not conducive to golf, the sport of green lushness manages to peek through, albeit in a perverse way.

*T*he age of excess has been fodder for the imagination of the modern cartoonist. Dana Summers shows how ridiculous "big everything" can be and Mike Peters's *Mother Goose and Grimm* probes "little everything" in the microworld.

MOTHER GOOSE AND GRIMM   BY MIKE PETERS   1989

PLUGGERS
BY JEFF MACNELLY
1993

The saga of Mary Worth began in 1932 as Apple Mary. It was the creation of Martha Orr. By 1940, the strip had been taken over by Allen Saunders, a professor of French, and Ken Ernst, a talented illustrator. Apple Mary became Mary Worth and the style of the strip became slicker and more modern, offering sage advice on everything from alcoholism, marital spats and golf. The strip is one of the most popular of all time as is testified to by its longevity.

Pluggers is the latest offering of multi-award-winning Jeff MacNelly. No sport demands the "plugging" attitude more than golf. Fortunately, most golfers are pluggers and old senior pluggers even seem to revel in it.

Neither rain, nor snow, nor dark of night, will stay a plugger from his appointed round

CROCK BY BILL RECHIN AND DON WILDER 1989

Reprinted with special permission of King Features Syndicate.

HAGAR THE HORRIBLE
BY DIK BROWNE
1992

GRIN & BEAR IT
BY LICHTY & WAGNER
1982

When General Dwight Eisenhower became president of the United States, the country was made aware that military men are infatuated with golf. It could be argued that striking the ball, driving it true to the target, serves to mentally reinforce the confidence of the striker (golfer) that he (or she) is still a mighty hunter, capable of fending off foes if necessary.

Mort Walker was drafted in 1943 and served in Italy during the war, working in intelligence. *Beetle Bailey* was banned from *The Stars and Stripes* for 10 years because it was disrespectful to officers.

Bill Rechin teamed up with author Don Wilder in 1975 to create *Crock*. During the Korean War, Rechin gained experience by doing training manuals. *Crock* reminds us that no matter where in the world we may find ourselves, it's still possible to get in a round of golf.

Richard "Dik" Browne began his career by covering the trial of Lucky Luciano. After a stint in the advertising world, where he created the Chiquita banana, he went on to win Reubens for *Hi and Lois* and *Hagar the Horrible*.

George "Lichty" Lichtenstein is one of the most irreverent cartoonists of all time, having been kicked out of college for hanging gags on Rembrandts that were on display at the school. *Grin & Bear It* began in 1932 and often had some wild words to say about golf.

"Here's the worst of it. . . Some of the golf carts at the club are becoming obsolete."

Reprinted with special permission of King Features Syndicate.

Brant Parker worked for the Binghampton Press in New York. In that capacity he was serving as a judge in an art contest that was won by Johnny Hart. What a serendipitous gift to the world, and the golfing world in particular. Their collaboration resulted in *The Wizard of Id*. The King of Id, a caustic, sardonic lovable curmudgeon and his lackey, Sir Rodney, have brought golf humor to a new high. Parker and Hart have both won the highest award for cartooning, the Reuben.

Since Clare Briggs, no strip has done more material on golf than *Hi and Lois*. Between Hi, his golfing buddy Fuzzy and their bewildered wives, we can all see ourselves with crystal clarity. After Dik died in 1989 the strip was taken over by his son, Chance, without any diminution of quality.

FRANK AND ERNEST   BY BOB THAVES   1983

Bill Hollbrook, in *On The Fast Track*, and Bob Thaves in *Frank and Ernest*, remind us that golfers must cope with the environment like everyone else. The United States Golf Association devotes much of its energy to making sure that golf will have a future in an environmentally stressed world.

THE MODERN
FAMILY STRIP

Ralph Dunagin and Dana Summers teamed up while working at the Orlando Sentinel to create their family strip, *The Middletons*. Throughout Dunagin's career, he has used golf as a background for his humor.

FoxTrot began in 1988. It was the creation of physicist-turned-cartoonist Bill Amend. Bill's early inspirations, when he lived in Newton, Massachusetts, came from *Mad Magazine*. Although he had the brains to get a degree in physics, his deep-seated love was cartooning. The family moved to the San Francisco Bay Area where Bill attended high school and made 8mm movies in his spare time. Bill plays golf in the cartoonist's tournament and the sport creeps into his strips each year. I think we can see the influence of *Mad* in the work shown here.

© 1980 Jim Unger/dist. by LaughingStock Licensing Inc.

"This shouldn't take too long!"

Doctors playing golf is as American as apple pie. In fact Wednesday has become the de facto "Doctor's day."

James Unger was born in London and was a cop, driving school instructor and auto repossessor at one time. He moved to Canada where he became an art director. In 1974, Universal Press took him on as a cartoonist. His tough, brash humor combined with his loose line style is something special. He has won the Reuben Award.

Bill Holbrook was born in Los Angeles, brought up in the South, went to Auburn and joined the staff of the *Atlanta Journal* as an editorial cartoonist in 1981. *Safe Havens* began publication in 1988 and often deals in a humorous way with serious subjects, as we see in the strip shown here.

FRANK AND ERNEST
BY BOB THAVES
1991

THE WIZARD OF ID
BY PARKER & HART
1988

©1993 Tribune Media Services, Inc.
All Rights Reserved

7-23

As we've seen in this book, the world of golf has made drastic changes over the last 100 years. Steve Moore and Wiley use humorous cynicism to put some of these changes in perspective.

Steve Moore was born in Denver but raised in La Cañada, California, with a cageful of snakes in his bedroom (a lot of his cartoons have snakes in them). He was sports editor for the *Maui Times* and decided to do a cartoon to add to the page. The result was *In the Bleachers*, which first appeared in 1985. Steve can make fun of golfers like no other.

"Nice follow-through, Hadley!"

THE NEIGHBORHOOD
BY JERRY VAN AMERONGEN
1981

Reprinted with special permission of King Features Syndicate.

One of the most exhilarating experiences in golf is the long drive. Power, power, power and more power. The styles of Jerry Van Amerongen and Jim Unger lend themselves perfectly to celebrate this experience.

Joe Martin, married with five sons and living in Wisconsin, began his career as an employment counselor. *Mister Boffo* is very much with the times and in what we see here, hopefully ahead of the times—way ahead.

J.C. Duffy brings an existential or Kafkaesque quality to his work. The individual is unique in a hostile world. Duffy forces you to think about golf and life.

HERMAN
BY JIM UNGER
1982

© 1982 Jim Unger/dist. by Laughingstock Licensing Inc.

"I was wondering how you'd play that shot."

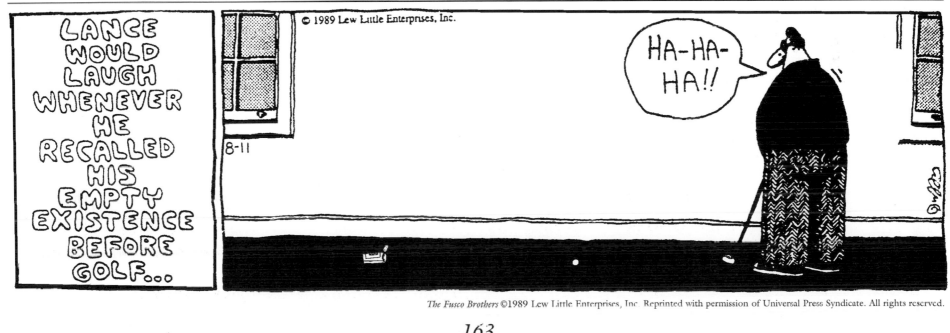

460 yards, par 4, dogleg right, blind approach, water hazard, bunkers... sheesh... sounds like my first marriage.

Kohlsaat

Relationships in the '90s are probably unique in the history of mankind. Peter Kohlsaat's *Single Slices* and Cathy Guisewite's *Cathy* give an insightful glimpse into this topic as it relates to golf.

Minnesota dentist-turned-cartoonist, Peter Kohlsaat is a freelance maverick in the comic strip business. Besides doing *Single Slices*, he does *The Nooz*, which he self-syndicates by sending postcards to newpaper editors or directly contacting them by driving around the country in his van with his dog Zelda at his side. His first love is fishing.

Cathy Guisewite, whose father was a stand-up comedian, has been doing *Cathy* since 1976. After graduating from the University of Michigan, Cathy worked as an advertising executive. Her strip adapts to the times and in the early '90s she produced a modest volume of work on golf that was really exceptional for its humor. She has dumped the real-life Irving (he's the golfer in the strip) and now lives in Los Angeles, where she is raising her young daughter. No information indicates that she plays golf—thank God!

GOLF IS

EXERCISE

Step aerobics for golfers

Those who claim that golfers aren't athletes know not of what they speak. Steve Moore and John McPherson clearly show that golfers must go through arduous exercise routines to maintain their "tone."

John McPherson discarded his engineering career to become a full time cartoonist. He actually recalls loving to draw on the family's walls as early as five, but didn't take the career up seriously until 20 years later. As anyone who is familiar with *Close to Home* might suspect, John's hobby is collecting bread-wrapper twist ties. The McPhersons live in Saratoga Springs, New York. I wonder if he collects broken tees?

Is Conrad telling us that Bill Clinton is trying to play golf with an instrument not designed for that purpose or is he simply saying the president swings a mean sax?

One of the most brilliant editorial cartoonists of our time is Paul Conrad. Conrad was born in 1924 in Cedar Rapids, Iowa. After serving in the army for five years, he began his career with the *Denver Post*. In 1964 he joined the *Los Angeles Times,* where he has been ever since. Conrad won the Pulitzer Prize in 1964 and in 1971.

According to the *USGA Golf Journal,* Clinton's handicap is in the low 20s. He is capable of cranking out long drives and is a good companion on the course, freely offering compliments to other players. The *Journal* states that Bill "scored in the 80s or low 90s depending on how many mulligans he took."

B. C.   BY JOHNNY HART   1989

Reprinted with special permission of King Features Syndicate.

Reprinted with special permission of King Features Syndicate.

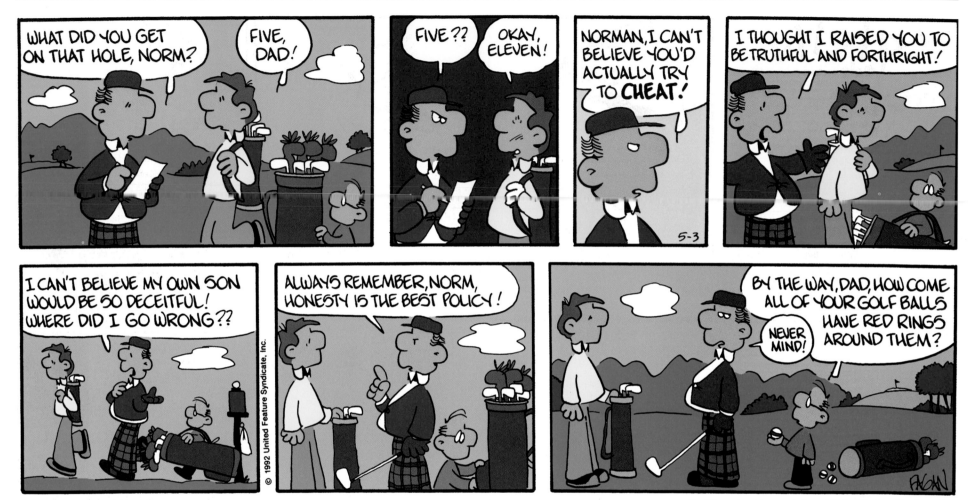

Drabble reprinted by permission of United Features Syndicate, Inc.

Kevin Fagan lives in southern California and loves to play golf. *Drabble* was created while Fagan was in college and began publication in 1979. Norman and his father Ralph are frequently on the links.

Bill Watterson created *Calvin and Hobbes* in 1985. It reflects on the fantasies of a six-year-old boy and his stuffed tiger, who comes to life when no one else is in the room. The strip has gained tremendous popularity. The names of the characters are derived from theologian John Calvin and philosopher Thomas Hobbes, reflecting Watterson's philosophical penchant.

The final pages of this book are dedicated to Mort Walker, Charles Schulz and Johnny Hart, whose innumerable contributions to golf humor are ineffable.

By permission of Johnny Hart and Creators Syndicate, Inc.

INDEX